The B.S. Boss Blueprint

A Guide to Perpetually Succeed

Dr. Lisa Lewis Ellis

ISBN: 978-1-7355265-2-2 (paperback)
ISBN: 978-1-7355265-3-9 (ebook)

Library of Congress Control Number: 2020917215

All scripture quotations, unless otherwise indicated, are taken from the New Living Translation version of the Bible.

Table of Contents

The B.S. Boss Blueprint

Welcome, welcome, welcome! I hope you have a pen and some paper, because I'm telling you *The B.S. Boss Blueprint* is going to change the game for you. I promise that it is going to change your life. Get comfortable. I'm Dr. Lisa Lewis Ellis, and I'm going to help you B.S. (Belief System) your way to success!

Let me start with a simple question: what is a blueprint? A blueprint is a detailed outline designed to get you from where you are today to where you want to be tomorrow.

The blueprint you hold in your hand is organized by guideposts. Each guidepost is intended to help construct a solid foundation on which you can build the life that you want. The guideposts are strategized to tackle one's belief systems, i.e., heart, soul, and mind. The hope is that by the end of the process, you're the boss of your B.S. and ultimately in control of your success going forward. You will be empowered and equipped to be the best version of yourself; to be you in all your gloriousness.

These chapters aren't long, and that is by design. They are to be thought-provoking, but not overwhelming. There is an area for you to take notes, but you are welcome to highlight or write in the margins at your leisure.

I was inspired to write this blueprint as a companion to my book, *Making B.S. Boss Moves: The Four R's to Achieving Success*, and as a standalone workbook for my coaching practice.

Now that the preliminaries are out of the way, I want to get into the good stuff.

In the *Americana* documentary on Netflix, Taylor Swift said that she had to deconstruct an entire belief system when she realized that she wasn't experiencing the level of success that she wanted in her professional life. She had to make an assessment of where she was and decided that the belief system she had been following wasn't serving her anymore. It wasn't supporting where she wanted to be and what she felt success was for her. Success is very personal. You have to think about what success looks and feels like to you, because success for you, Taylor Swift and even myself are very different things. What does success look like, feel like, smell like to you? To figure this out, Taylor Swift had to deconstruct her entire belief system, and we're going to do some of that as well.

First, what is a belief system? According to study.com, "a belief system is an ideology or set of principles that help us to interpret our everyday reality. This could be in the form of religion, political affiliation, philosophy, or spirituality, among many other things. These beliefs are shaped and influenced by several different factors." You see, everything goes into a belief system- spirituality, philosophy, politics, everything. We're constantly getting voices that are coming in and helping build our belief system. We get them from childhood all the way up until adulthood, from our college, our political affiliation, our church affiliation, our friends; we get them from all over. All of these things are woven together, and they become the fibre of what we think and how we move around in the Earth.

According to Collins Dictionary, "the belief system of a person or society is the set of beliefs that they have about what is right and wrong and what is true and false." So, part of a belief system can revolve around whether or not we believe it's right or wrong to rob a bank, for example. I think most of us don't think it's right. However, we still get conflicted sometimes. What if someone is stealing groceries from the grocery store because they don't have enough money to feed themselves. They don't have access to any other resources and they're hungry. Or worse: they have children that they aren't able to feed. When you throw in these other factors, there's some compassion that wells up in us.

This challenges the belief system that says stealing is wrong. It's still wrong, but if we encounter an individual that is in dire circumstances, we may actually pay for the groceries ourselves. Then the store owner may say that since the groceries were actually paid for, they will let the thief go with a warning not to come back. Our belief system says it's wrong, but there are other variables that come into play that may cause us to lean and be a little empathetic and sympathetic.

So how does that tie into *The B.S. Boss Blueprint*? We have to look at and dig deeper into what it is we believe in. Is it so firmly fixed that there's no wiggle room? And when we realize we're not where we want to be, are we going to be able to bulldoze our beliefs? That's what deconstruction is. That's what Taylor Swift had to do; break it all down and tear it all up.

Now for a question you've probably been wondering: who am I? I'm Dr. Lisa Lewis Ellis, the B.S. Boss. I teach individuals and groups how to release self-limiting belief systems to achieve personal success and prosperity. I am an Amazon bestselling author, and I've been seen in *Black Enterprise* and the *New York Times*. I also regularly contribute periodicals and blog posts all over the web. My most recent book is *Today I Choose Me From Empty Nest to Full Throttle*, which is available on amazon.com. I'm also a certified, personal and executive coach in positive psychology. I'm skilled in the strength survey and the strength binders, which are the Gallup strength finders. I bring a wealth of tools to the table.

I also have thirty-one years of experience in leadership and management in the public financial sector. In my other life, I am known as the money lady, because I control the purse. I'm also a John Maxwell Team-certified coach, teacher, speaker, and trainer. And the 'doctor' in my title refers to my honorary degree, a doctorate in divinity. I'm also ordained clergy in the Christian faith. So, I bring all that good stuff to you.

So that is who I am, and now you know that the person sharing information with you is not crazy. Right? Well, now that this is all out of the way, let's get into our first guidepost.

Guidepost One

Chapter 1

Heart

"Guard your heart above all else, for it determines the course of your life." Proverbs 4:23 (New Living Translation)

According to Dictionary.com, heart is defined as, [3]the center of the total personality, especially with reference to intuition, feeling, or emotion, [4]the center of emotion, especially as contrasted to the head as the center of the intellect, [5]capacity for sympathy; feeling; affection, [6]spirit, courage, or enthusiasm, [7]the innermost or central part of anything, and [8]the vital or essential part; core.

Any time I want to do something outside of the norm, take something to the next level, or try something new, I have learned to do a heart check. The heart is my core, intuition, emotions, and feeling about the "thing." If my heart isn't pure about it then I unpack my reasons.

Case in point: What you're holding in your hand is "next level" for me. When I completed and submitted the manuscript for *Making B.S. Boss Moves: The Four R's to*

3

Achieving Success, I couldn't sleep. That is not normal for me. When I complete a project that I know was divinely inspired, I typically let out a sigh of relief and rest easy. I feel a sense of accomplishment and contentment because I succeeded at completing the task at hand. Not so in this case.

In fact, I wasn't sleeping well at night because this blueprint that you are holding in your hand – combination guide and workbook – kept nagging at me; it had to be written. I mean, n-a-g-g-i-n-g at me. I **love** my sleep. So, when something keeps me up, I do a deep-dive investigation. I try to determine what's keeping me up and address it so I can enjoy my sleep.

Sleep was elusive because I needed to write this guide to be released, if not simultaneously with the book, shortly thereafter. To put it into context for you, that means that I wrote two books in less than thirty days. Who does that? God, what are you doing to me?

I had to check my heart. Was it a matter of economics that was driving me to write the companion book? "No." Was it to be braggadocious about writing two full books in less than thirty days? "No, that's not my character or personality." My writing was for no other reason than God inspiring me to do so. My core motive was pure.

As we journey together through *The B.S. Boss Blueprint: A Guide to Perpetually Succeed,* a heart check is vital to accomplishing your life's goals successfully. Ask yourself the hard questions and answer yourself honestly.

I often say: "You can lie to everybody else, but please tell yourself the truth." This journey requires truth. It requires a pure heart and pure motives at the very core of who you are.

Let's get this party started!

Chapter 2

Believe

*H*ow can we put success on repeat with God? We are going to dig into the Scriptures, so grab your Bible.

Guidepost One has to do with what we believe and how that supports putting success on repeat. Jeremiah 29:11 in *The Message Bible* reads: "I, God, know what I'm doing. I have it all planned out, plans to take care of you, not abandon you, plans to give you the future you hope for." Now, I love *The Message Bible* translation, because it breaks it down into very plain terms for me and helps me understand. With this clearer language, we can extrapolate the text and see how God has a plan for us to perpetually succeed. It's consistent with the word of God.

Point One – God knows what God is doing.

That's what it says the first part of Jeremiah 29 in *The Message Bible*, "I, God, know what I am doing." God knows what God is doing. I think that's important to mention because sometimes when we have a plan, and there's an idea that is in our heart and in our spirit, we get lost. We get off track. We get discouraged because things come up that will derail and distract us. This may throw us off course, but we have to remind ourselves that God knows what God is doing. He would not have given us that vision or that goal if he did not know what he was doing, right? Oh, that's some good stuff right there.

Point Two – God has a complete plan and blueprint.
When God was talking to Jeremiah, Jeremiah said to God: "You can't be calling me. You can't mean for me to do this." Jeremiah talked about the fact that he was too young to do what God had called him to do. He didn't feel like he was equipped to do the assignment that God had given him. Don't you see us in that? I know I see myself. There have been things that God asked me to do, and I immediately started the negative self-talk and trying to disqualify myself.

"Oh no," I would tell myself, "I can't do that. I don't have the time. I may not have the skill set or I don't have a full understanding. You can't possibly mean me, God, right?" I'm no different from Jeremiah.

Another saint that comes to mind in this instance is Moses. When Moses was called by God to go to Pharaoh and tell Pharaoh to let his people go, Moses gave every excuse in the book. "Who can I say sent me? I'm slow of speech. I can't do this. Okay, fine." God had a rebuttal for everything Moses came up with, because He has a complete plan- a complete blueprint from beginning to end. If I think about every time I've come up with a reason why I could not do something or why I felt like an assignment was too big for me to accomplish, God had to remind me as he did Jeremiah, saying: "Look, I know the plans that I have for you."

God has a complete plan and a blueprint from the very beginning. He would not have even put it in our hearts or given us the idea if he didn't know that we could complete the assignment. He has equipped us; He knows what's inside us. All he's doing is allowing that's within us to come out by giving us assignments and projects. Isn't that good stuff right there? That's the kind of stuff that makes me excited every time I think about it; that God has a complete plan. He doesn't do anything halfway.

Think about the creation. In Genesis, when it says: "God said." Now, God didn't say and just leave it hanging out there, right? He didn't just say and leave it on pause. He spoke that thing into existence and it happened- completely, fully, and lacking nothing.

God having a plan doesn't mean that it's all going to be smooth, however. It doesn't mean that we won't come up against any bumps in the road. God did not say that every day would be sunny and there would be no rain. He did not promise there would be no trials or tribulations. That's not what God said; that's not consistent with scripture. What is consistent is that God is with us through it all, and he will see us through because he has a complete blueprint and a complete plan.

Point three – God's plan is to take care of us and to not abandon us. Let me say that again. **God's plan is to take care of you and not abandon you**. Why is that important for us when we talk about a blueprint or guide? When we talk about perpetual success, it's important to know that God doesn't give us an assignment in order to fail. He doesn't give us this calling and this charge to leave us out there by ourselves and abandon us. He is with us.

We put our hand in God's, and he is there with us and for us, taking care of us every single step of the way. He is not going to leave us drained or flapping out in the wind. Regardless of the trial and the tribulation, God is there. He is with us to take care of us and to not abandon us. Hallelujah!

When I think about how God takes care of us, I immediately think about a song that I learned as a child. It's one that almost everybody knows. "He's Got the Whole World in His Hands."

The scripture tells us in Isaiah that the Earth is God's footstool. He's got the whole world in his hands. This world is turning on its axis right now, as you're reading this book; it is rotating and none of us are falling off. Your chair isn't lifting and floating around; gravity is holding us to the ground. God is in control of everything. It is not his desire or his plan to abandon us. His desire is that we succeed in accomplishing the goals that he put inside our heart.

Point Four – God desires to give us the future we hope for. There are doors set before us, and we have options. We have places to go and things to do. That thing that is in our heart, the desire that he placed on the inside of us, it is his desire to give that thing to us. That's what Jeremiah 29:11 declares for us. Perpetually succeeding, being able to put success on repeat, is knowing that it's God's desire to do good by us.

This picture of my daughter and I with the camels in early 2020 captured a desire in our hearts. It was our goal and our desire to go to Dubai. We had that thing inside us, and finally, we stepped out in faith and made the necessary plans to make it happen. When I went to Dubai, I said there were several things I was going to do, one of which was ride a camel. Here I am on the camel, with my daughter is leading me around.

That is God. That is Jeremiah 29:11 in action, demonstrated in my life. How is God showing up and demonstrating in your own life? With a plan to help you perpetually succeed. God doesn't play favorites. He doesn't favor me, my daughter, or my family any more than he favors you; He loves you.

What is the desire that is in your heart? What is that thing that you want to do? I am living proof, here to tell you that it is God's desire to give you that thing. Oh, my God. He has a plan for us to perpetually succeed. Oh, my God. Thank you, Lord Jesus.

What does success look like for you? That picture is what success looked like for me for that particular vision

I had for my life at that time. You are the success story. I am God's success story. We are a demonstration of God- of God's love. We are the demonstration of God knowing us before we were formed in our mother's womb. Your testimony, your life, is what's going to cause others to want to know what they must do to be saved. They will desire a relationship with this God that had such a plan and an idea for your life, and that he has for their life.

Again, not every day is going to be rosy. Some rain is going to fall, some storms are going to come. Some trials are going to show up- disappointments, setbacks, and disturbances. He has a plan and he knows what he's doing from beginning to end.

When we get discouraged, we've got to remind ourselves of what he's telling us in Jeremiah 29:11. First and foremost, God knows what God is doing. Second, God has a complete plan and a blueprint for what he's doing for us, with us, and through us. We can trust in that and we can trust God. The third point is that his plan is to take care of us and not abandon us. We are not in this alone. We are not in this by ourselves. God is with us in the trenches.

It's just like Shadrach, Meshach, and Abednego. When they went into the fiery flames in the fiery furnace, they said: "If we go, we're going to go. We believe that God will take us out of here, but even if he doesn't, amen, we know that God is with us." To be absent from the body is to be present with God. We are on a mission, and His plan is so that we can perpetually succeed, giving him glory and honor, and pointing others toward God.

Fourth and final, his plan is to give us the future that we hope for, that he put inside us. Glory to God.

Chapter 3

Reassess

*N*ow that we've discussed what's in our heart and what we believe, it's time to do some work. The next thing that we're going to get into is the steps that we take toward our belief system.

Our way to success is by reassessing. We must reassess our belief systems to compare and contrast where we are, where we want to be, and what success looks like. We've got to take a deep, good look. That's why the magnifying glass is there; this is not surface work. We've got to go in with the magnifying glass. To reassess means to estimate or judge the value or character of a thing, situation, or circumstance.

'Reassess' is synonymous with 'appraising' and 'adjusting.' So, think about an appraisal. If you've ever bought a house, part of the house-buying process is the mortgage company sending an appraiser to determine the value of the house. If that house doesn't value at the amount the individual is trying to sell for, then the mortgage company is going to make the seller bring the price down to the appraised amount.

Reassess your belief system's current value. What is the appraised value and where's the gap in the middle? If it's not serving you, it's not very valuable.

We have to evaluate that. If our belief system is not serving us or getting us where we want to go, it has a negative value. So, we have to change it. And that's the importance of the reassess.

What came up for you as your read about "reassess?" Make a list here of belief systems that need reassessment. This is your safe space. I'm not even going to limit you with lines. Just let it flow and pour out onto the page.

Chapter 4

Renovate

*N*ow that we've reassessed and determined that we've got to make some changes, we're ready to take the next step in the process, which is to renovate.

Coming back to the home-buying analogy, imagine a house in the middle of a renovation. What does it conjure up for you, if you've ever been part of a renovation project or building of a new home? It likely brings angst and heartache, but it's necessary to tear it down in order to build it up again. You have to get down to the bones.

Have you ever had flooding in your house? I think about the time I went to buy a new home. It was newly constructed, and I was super excited about it. When we went in to do the home inspection, the inspector filled the bathtub and turned on the jets. Then we moved around into other parts of the house. While we were in the basement, we hear like a little *shhh* sound, like water moving. We follow the sound to the part of the basement that's under the master bathroom, and there is water falling everywhere. It was coming out of the sprinkler system, and out of the smoke alarm. It was just everywhere, like an indoor rainstorm! We run upstairs and turn off the jets off. Obviously, something was installed incorrectly.

When I talk to the builder and told him my son had respiratory challenges, and that in order for me to purchase this home, I needed the drywall to come down and the carpet to come up. There was water everywhere, and I needed some renovation and some mold remediation. I didn't know if it was the first time the tub had leaked like that, and mold can grow quickly if you don't get to it fast enough.

It was going to involve a renovation of an already brand-new house. But guess what? It was necessary for me to go back to the reassessment, to realize it was valuable for it to be taken care of before I signed on the dotted line. I didn't take on that expense; I didn't take on that responsibility.

To renovate means to restore to good condition; make new, or as if new again; to repair. So, to renovate the belief system, we've first reassessed it. Now, we're at the place where we're tearing it apart because we need to make it new. Renovate it, refresh it, revive it, renew it, in order for it to serve us in our achieving success.

And by the way, the seller agreed to do certain things, but not everything that I needed done. So, I didn't purchase that house. I ended up getting a different house, but that speaks to the importance of the renovation process. If we can't get it to the place where it begins to serve us, then maybe it's time for something new or different. That's the importance of the renovation process.

What came up for you as your read about "renovate?" Make a list of belief systems that need renovating. This is your safe space. I'm not even going to limit you with lines. Just let it flow and pour out onto the page.

Chapter 5

S.H.I.F.T.

At this point in the process, we have dealt with what is in our heart. We've taken a magnifying glass to what we believe- not in theory, but in practice. We have reassessed and renovated what hasn't been working.

That gets us in a position to S.H.I.F.T. our belief system as necessary. We now have

Strategic, Highly-Intentional, Fulfilling Truths.

We not only believe what's possible, we now know all things are possible.

S.H.I.F.T

STRATEGIC
HIGHLY
INTENTIONAL
FULFILLING
TRUTHS

2
RENOVATE

1
REASSESS

BELIEVE

● Heart

Guidepost Two

Chapter 6

Soul

"In the same way, wisdom is sweet to your soul. If you find it you will have a bright future, and your hopes will not be cut short." Proverbs 24:14 (New Living Translation)
Dictionary.com
4the emotional part of human nature; the seat of the feelings or sentiments.
Soul is synonymous with courage, genius, spirit, and vitality.

*I*t isn't by mistake that soul work comes into play when talking about achieving success. It takes courage, genius, spirit, and vitality to make a dream come true. There will be obstacles, because that's how life is. There are ups and downs, ebbs and flows. If goal attainment were easy, everybody would be doing it, not just talking about it or daydreaming. To take the next steps in our journey together, we have to keep our head out of the clouds. We have to stay grounded and at one with our emotions, feelings, and sentiments.

How does soul work look? Well, let me use writing this book as an example.

The soul work I had to do for this project was to be honest with myself that I didn't want to write the book. No – I – did – not! I was so glad to finish *B.S. Boss Moves* that I wanted to throw myself an "It's Finished!" party. But before I set the date or ordered any noisemakers, this book was moving in my soul and spirit.

I wasn't feeling this book. However, it's my heart's desire to do what God inspires me to do when God inspires me to do it. I had very candid conversations with God too, trying to negotiate doing this project at a much, much, much later date. I still couldn't sleep, so my negotiating techniques weren't working on a divine level.

As a clergywoman, I have vowed to serve God by serving His creation. God gently reminded me that this book is meant to serve and help and inspire His creation. It's not about me and my tiredness. It's not about me and wanting to wait until next year. Someone needs this now; not next year, but this year. It would appear that God's negotiating techniques are far more persuasive.

The book you're holding in your hands is a direct result of my soul work. The soul work is going to be critical in taking the next steps.

Chapter 7

Create

*W*e're going to look at the story of Joseph and see what we can glean from his life and his experience. Grab your Bibles and turn to Genesis 50:19.

Just in case you are not be familiar with Joseph, let me give you a little bit of backstory. Joseph was part of a large family. He had several brothers, but due to being the youngest, he was the apple of his father's eye. His father loved them all equally, but he had a little something special for Joseph.

One day, Joseph had a dream. In this dream, he saw the stalks bowing down to him. When he sought God and asked him for an interpretation of what that dream meant, God revealed to him that it meant his brothers would one day bow down to him; that he would someday be in a position of authority.

Well, Joseph being the innocent younger brother that he was, he shared that dream with his brothers. To say that they were angry, incensed, and jealous is an understatement. They were so angry at the story that one day, when they were out hunting together, they left him out there. They dug a pit and dropped him in, leaving him for dead. If that wasn't enough, they took his clothing, which they rolled around in the blood of an animal and took back to their father, saying: "Dad, we don't know how to explain this to you, but Joseph was taken by some animals and this is all that is left." Their father was devastated. It broke him spiritually.

Well, because God is not a liar and had given Joseph that dream, there happened to be some passers-by that heard Joseph. They found him and pulled him out of the pit, but unfortunately, he ended up in slavery.

Now here was this young man; he had done nothing, and he was in slavery. His brothers were so jealous and angry about the vision that God had given him, but this wasn't something that Joseph had wanted. This was something that God had dropped in his spirit, and that's important for us to know. Joseph ended up in prison and he went from the pit to the prison, and- eventually- to the palace.

Joseph got to the palace because of an encounter that he had in prison with the cup bearer. While he was in prison, he was interpreting dreams and giving prophetic words of encouragement to those that were imprisoned. And the cup bearer, in particular, he told: "Look, when you get back to work and you get on the outside, remember me. Don't forget about me." When the cup bearer eventually left and was back working in the palace, he absolutely forgot about Joseph. Sometimes, that's what happens.

However, at some point, the king had a dream. He had had this dream repeatedly over several nights, but he couldn't interpret its meaning. So, he asked everyone in his employ if they knew of anyone who could interpret his dream. And then, as God would have it, the cup bearer remembered the encounter with Joseph and he let the king know, saying: "I know somebody! I know someone who was able to interpret dreams, and who hears from God, and who was able to give a prophetic word."

Immediately, the king says: "Well, bring him to me!"

"Oh, but the person is in jail."

"Not a problem. I'm the king. Go get him out of jail. Bring him to me because I need an interpretation of this dream."

Of course, Joseph was able to interpret the King's dream. In the dream, God was giving the king instructions on how they should store up grain, food, money, and other resources because a time of famine was going to come. According to the dream, there was going to be seven years of feasting and abundance, followed by seven years of harsh famine. God was giving the king instructions on what to do for his household and for the entire kingdom so that they would get through the famine successfully.

This is where we come in with Genesis 50:19.

"Joseph replied, 'Don't be afraid. Do I act for God? Don't you see, you planned evil against me, but God used those same plans for my good. As you see all around you right now, life for many people, easy now. You have nothing to fear. I'll take care of you and your children.' He reassured them, speaking to them heart-to-heart."

When we pick up this story in Genesis 50:19-21, the famine has come. Joseph is in a position of authority as a reward for rightly interpreting the dream that the king had. The king saw him as an honorable man, a godly man, and he put him in this position. It's equivalent to being the president and the vice president. In this case, Joseph was in the position of being the vice president. So, he had all this oversight and authority, and Joseph was put in charge of storing up the resources in preparation for the famine.

So, the season of famine arrived, and Joseph's brothers came into the town city, wanting to speak to the king or whoever was in charge. Back home, they didn't get word that Joseph had become right-hand man to the king. And they didn't do what the king had done and stored up during those seven years. So, Joseph's brothers came into town, looking for whoever was in charge, saying: "Look, we need help. We are hungry. People are dying. We are in the midst of a famine and we need some resources. We understand that there are resources here, and we would like to get our family's portion, our rations."

They didn't even realize, initially, that the person that they were speaking to was their brother- the brother they had left for dead. Joseph recognized them immediately, because he asked them: "Where do you come from? Who is your father and your mother?" When they answered him, they confirmed that they were indeed his brothers.

Then after Joseph had asked all these questions, it dawned on his brothers who they were standing in front of, which is why Joseph said to them, "Don't be afraid." This is because when his brothers realized who he was, and that he had not died in the wilderness as they had planned, Joseph was in a position in which he could have exacted revenge.

With that, let's get to our first lesson.

Point One – Not everyone will recognize and acknowledge God's plan for your life and your success.

Look at Joseph's story. These were his brothers, his blood relation. They chose not to recognize or acknowledge God's plan for his life and for his success, or that it was to everyone's benefit. So, in a rage of jealousy, they plotted evil against him.

Our first lesson is to know that not everybody will recognize it. We often can't help but be disappointed and disheartened when those that we love or people that we think would want to encourage and support us don't recognize your path to success. God gave that vision, that dream, to Joseph; he didn't give it to his brothers. The dream, the idea that is in your spirit, that God has dropped in your heart, is something that he has given to you. Not everybody will support it; Joseph's own brothers didn't support it. Yet, because God is not a liar, He was certain that the dream that He had given him would come to pass.

It's the same thing for you today. If you're feeling discouraged because those that you thought would support you aren't doing so, I'm here to tell you the word from God is that, whatever has been given to you, it's from God. Amen. Keep working at it.

Point two – Flip the script, because God's plan prevails.

Joseph told his brothers: "Look, don't be afraid," because they realized who he was. They realized that he was not dead. And there it was, decades later, and they were standing in front of him. In essence, they were bowing down to him, just like what Joseph had seen in the dream that they were so angry about. Yet still he said: "Look, don't be afraid. Don't worry. I'm not here to exact revenge. God did not put me in this position to exact revenge on you."

He told them: "Don't you see? What you planned for evil, what you planned to destroy me and used against me, God turned it around for my good." God flipped the script because God's plan prevails. So, when you look at your life today, there may be some moments in which God flipped the script, because He prevails. And if that script has not been flipped yet, you can bet that God is turning that thing around. What you thought would destroy you is actually going to bless you. What you thought would take you down will actually lift you up and promote you.

That's exactly what happened with Joseph. He was in a pit, then prison, and God used these things to promote him. I don't know what pits have been in your life. I don't know what prisons you have found yourself in, be they physical, spiritual, emotional, or mental. God can take that thing and turn it around.

Point three – God's plan will bless you and others.

God is not one dimensional. God is not selfish. God is not blessing you. He's not blessing me. He's not blessing us for our own benefit. We can enjoy it, but he's blessing us to be a blessing.

Back to the scripture. After Joseph told his brothers how God had flipped the script, he said to them: "As you see all around you right now, life for many people easy now. You have nothing to fear. You have nothing to fear. I'll take care of you and your children."

God has blessed Joseph so that he could bless his family and his household. God has blessed you so that you can be a blessing unto others. God is enlarging your territory and giving you that idea or witty inventions which may provide for yourself and others. So, God's plan will bless you so that you may bless others.

Point four – Take care of your heart and the heart of others.

What does that mean, Dr. Lisa? What that means is if you go back to the last part of Genesis 50:19-21, it says: "Speaking with them, he reassured them." Joseph spoke with them, heart-to-heart. There's a place in the Scripture which states that out of the abundance of the heart, the mouth speaks. So, he is speaking to them from a point of wholeness, healthiness, forgiveness, love, and peace. We have to take care of our heart so that we may care for the hearts of others.

Joseph, the individual that was hurt by evil, he was in a position to be able to either bless them or curse them. Since God had taken care of Joseph's heart, he was able to care for those who would have had nothing better but for him to die and be killed. So, the lesson is to allow God to take care of our heart. We're on assignment to bless others. We must take care of our heart so that we can care for the hearts of others. Amen.

Chapter 8

Redefine

$\mathcal{T}$he next step in our blueprint is to redefine. You see the pattern, yet? Reassess, renovate, redefine. We need to repair and reinvigorate our belief systems. So, to make it fresh, we've got to redefine it.

We've got to get in there and decide on what it means to us. Remember, your definition of success is different than mine in terms of how it's materialized and what it looks like. For you, success may be buying a new home. For me, it may be downsizing into a smaller place. So, we must redefine what success is and what our belief system is.

"Business as usual" hasn't gotten you where you want to be in terms of achieving your goals. Just because it worked then, that doesn't mean it's going to work now. "Business as usual" is not allowing us to tick off our goals and our achievements. So, we got to put a stop to it, no more business as usual. We've got to redefine success and determine what it looks like at this stage of our journey.

A good example of that is the belief that a woman's place is at home in the kitchen. This is not something I believe, but we're going to pretend that it is, just for the sake of example. If my belief system dictates that a woman's place is in the kitchen, that's it. She can't be a professional, she can't run a company, she can't work outside the home. Yet, I have a personal goal of independence that doesn't fit into this belief. I have to redefine that belief system. I made a reassessment, which told me that what I'm believing right now is not getting me to the independence I crave. Next, I renovated that system and tore it apart. Now I have to redefine it to fit my dream. Redefining this system may cause me to realize that I don't really want to work outside the home because I want to be here with the kids.

How can I make that happen? After redefining it, I still want my independence, even if I don't want to leave my kids. I want financial independence and no longer have to rely on an allowance of some sort. So, what does that look like?

That looks like me working from home by finding something that I can do for a living without having to leave the house. There it is, simple as that. What I just did just now was reconsider and reformulate what my personal success looked like. I wanted the financial independence, but I also wanted the flexibility of being able to be at home with the children, and that led me to discover working from home as my heart's desire.

What came up for you as your read about "redefine?" Make a list here of belief systems that need redefining. This is your safe space. I'm not even going to limit you with lines. Just let it flow and pour out onto the page.

Chapter 9

Reaffirm

*T*he fourth part of soul work is to reaffirm. According to dictionary.com, to reaffirm is "to assert solemnly; to express agreement with or commitment to upholding support." And it is synonymous with "approve, endorse, advocate, proclaim, and repeat." Do you see a pattern where I see a pattern? We have reassessed, we have renovated, we have redefined, and now we're at the place where we're going to reaffirm. It's important to do at this point, because it's around now that most people lose their drive.

It always happens. It never fails. When we have decided that this is the route we're going to take in order to achieve success, something always happens to discourage, derail, and/or distract us; to take us back to "businesses as usual." To use the previous chapter's example, when we look for the work-from-home job to gain financial independence, we may get frustrated. That's normal.

I can't tell you how frustrated I was that the builder wouldn't make all the changes and repairs that I asked for, because I really did like that house. I was so disappointed. I had to repeat to myself what I wanted in a home and the reason why I was looking for a new build. I had to reaffirm that- not to the builder, not to my real-estate agent, but to myself. Despite all the forces that would derail or distract me, I had to reaffirm my goals and advocate for myself.

When you begin to B.S. your way to success, you're going to have to advocate for yourself. You are going to have to proclaim to yourself and to others the success you are working toward and stand in your truth.

Taylor Swift had to deconstruct her belief system. Now, she owns her own music. When she realized that the record company owned the music she made and could do what they wanted to do with it- release it however they wanted to, tell her she couldn't sing certain songs at certain concerts, and more – that's when she learned that she wasn't in control of her own success. So, in advocating for herself, reassessing, renovating, redefining, and then reaffirming, she's now signed with a new label that is in alignment with her belief system. Now, her music is a whole new sound. It's so liberated and independent because she had to reaffirm and advocate for herself with the company and with her music. She is her product. You are your own success, remember?

Keep in mind the synonyms of reaffirm – to prove, endorse, advocate, proclaim, repeat.

What came up for you as your read about "reaffirm?" Make a list here of belief systems that need reaffirming. This is your safe space. I'm not even going to limit you with lines. Just let it flow and pour out onto the page.

Chapter 10

S.E.R.V.E.

At this point in the process, we have dealt with what is in our soul. We've taken a magnifying glass to our emotions and examined what we've been practicing up to this point in our lives. We have redefined and reaffirmed what success is for us, individually – not what others say success is. Our words have power, and our actions are a demonstration of our words.

That gets us in a position to S.E.R.V.E. our belief systems, as necessary. We now

Support Effective, Repeatable, Victorious Experiences. We want it, we create it; co-create it with God.

S.E.R.V.E

SUPPORT
EFFECTIVE
REPEATABLE
VICTORIOUS
EXPERIENCES

4 REAFFIRM

3 REDEFINE

CREATE

● Soul

Guidepost Three

Chapter 11

Mind

"From a wise mind comes wise speech; the words of the wise are persuasive." Proverbs 16:23 (New Living Translation)

Dictionary.com

[6]intellectual power or ability

[8]a way of thinking and feeling; disposition; temper

[10]opinion, view, or sentiments

[11]inclination or desire

[12]purpose, intention, or will

[16]attention; thoughts

*M*ind is synonymous with attitude, desire, determination, mood, will, and wish, to name only a few words. We have laid a firm foundation on which to build our success. We have put pillars in place to hold up the framing and the house of accomplishment. We are now at the place where our mind has to be ready and right. The way we think at this point is everything. If we think we can't reach the goal, we won't. No need to mince words at this juncture of our journey together. I'm not biting my tongue, and I'm certainly not stuttering.

To successfully finish this book, I had to get my way of thinking and feeling right. My desire to sleep and to please God – maybe not quite in that order – dominated my thoughts. My purpose, intention, and disposition overrode my tiredness. I didn't get my divine intellectual power and ability until I started to write. The thoughts were coming to my mind faster than my fingers could move across the keyboard. There are parts of this book that were coming so fast I had to speak them into a recorder and transcribe them later.

The trajectory to success is such that once we're all in – heart, soul, and mind – not much can stop us. I used to enjoy riding roller coasters. The higher, the better. More loops on the track? Bring it on. Getting our mindset right is like riding a roller coaster. Not much can stop a roller coaster once it gets rolling. Nothing but an emergency brake.

We must have our mind right, because the closer we get to the goal line, the easier it is to want to throw in the towel. We remind ourselves that we are finishers, not quitters. Trust me, if you've gotten this far in the book, you're not a quitter. You – are – a – finisher.

I am proud of you. Go for the gold!

Chapter 12

Manifest

*W*e are going to be reading in 1 Chronicles 28:11-19 of
The Message Bible. It is quite a bit of reading, but I
tell you, it's going to be worth it. It reads as follows:

"Then David presented his son Solomon with the plans
for The Temple complex, porch, storerooms, meeting
rooms, and the place for atoning sacrifice. He turned over
the plans for everything that God's Spirit had brought to
his mind, the design of the courtyards, the arrangements
of rooms, and the closets for storing all the holy things. He
gave him his plan for organizing the Levites and priests
in their work of leading and ordering worship in the house
of God, and for caring for the liturgical furnishings. He
provided exact specifications for how much gold and silver
was needed for each article used in the services of worship, the gold and the silver lampstands and lamps, the
gold tables for consecrated bread, the silver tables, the
gold forks, the bowls and the jars, and the Incense Altar,
and he gave him the plan for sculpting the cherubs with
their wings outstretched over the Chest of the Covenant
of God, the cherubim throne. 'Here are the blueprints for

the whole work, for the whole project as God gave me to understand it,' David said."

Look at David's story and how God had given him a divine download, as I like to call it, on the temple and how He wanted everything done. David knew that his time was not necessarily coming to an end, but it was important for him to pass on what God had given him to the next generation.

Point one – God gives us plans which are for legacy builders – those willing to do the work.

If we're not going to do the work, put in the time, or make the necessary sacrifices after God gives us that divine download, then guess what? We don't have a plan to perpetually succeed.

In fact, the plan is not going to succeed, and there's no way that it can, because it is about building a legacy for those that are willing to do the work. If we are not about building a legacy for our loved ones or passing it along to the next generation so they can pass it to the next generation, then there's no reason for God to waste His time and give us a plan. That said, I'm here to tell you that there is a plan for you. God has a divine download for you. God has given you an assignment and told you what He needs you to do, but again, it's not just for you – it's for legacy builders.

Point Two – God is in the details.

Next, David passed the details on to Solomon. The scripture tells us that God is in the details. Imagine a fingerprint; your fingerprints. Have you ever had your fingerprints taken? I have. I've had my fingerprints taken several times for different jobs, and no single fingerprint is exactly alike. Even identical twins do not have the same exact fingerprint.

Look at the snowflake analogy. I don't know if you've had snow where you are. I'm in the Washington D.C. area, and we get snow. Just imagine seeing a snowflake and knowing that no two are alike. That is a reminder and a clear illustration that God is in the details.

There was a deep level of intricacy that God gave David in terms of the temple, because this was the place that they were coming to worship Him. When God does a divine download, it's for legacy builders and those willing to do the work. He gives us blow-by-blow details. He gives us enough. We may not always see the end or the final product, but He gives us enough to know God is in the details. He doesn't make mistakes. God is in the details. He knows what we'll encounter when we go straight. He knows what we'll encounter when we go right. He knows what we'll encounter when we go left. He is in the details because He knows the outcome.

God knows what the finished product is going to look like. He knows what success looks like for you and I. He has a vision. He gives us the details we need to know so it can come out the way that He designed it. If we don't think that God is in the details, look at Genesis 1. In the creation of the universe, He called things out and separated things. If we want to take part in God's plan to perpetually succeed, we must acknowledge and accept that God is in the details.

I think about being a mom of two adults, and how when I give them instructions, they're amazed at the detail that

I provide them. I tell them it's because God loves them so much, and I, knowing that God is in the details, provide a confirmation that I have in fact heard from God on their behalf. God is in the details, and plans are for legacy builders – those individuals that will not only build but pass it along.

Point Three – the Holy Spirit inspires, influences, and helps.

When Jesus was baptized and he came up out of the water, it said that a dove descended upon Him, and the light of God shone on Him. They heard the voice of God say: "This is my beloved Son in whom I am well pleased." So, when God gives the divine download, He doesn't just throw it at us and tell us to do the best that we can. Absolutely not. We have Holy Spirit. Holy Spirit is there to inspire us, influence us, hover over us, and help us to achieve the plan and the goals that God has given us in the divine download. The Holy Spirit is helping us every step of the way so that we may succeed and get to where God would have us be.

You are not alone; that is a trick of the devil.

That is a trick of the enemy to make you think you are in this by yourself. You are not. You have God, who has given the divine download. You have the Holy Spirit inside you, and your heavenly host that is able to help you. We have help.

None of us are helpless. We have the Holy Spirit inspiring us, influencing us, and – best of all – helping us. Amen.

Point Four – Know when and how to pass the plan along.

That is important because as I mentioned earlier, David, to whom God had given the divine download, had given all the specifications on how to build the temple. In 1 Chronicles, when God instructed David to build the temple, He even told them who to get. Craftsmen who were skilled in different areas, that they would bring their skills. The scripture even talks about individuals that were anointed.

In the Old Testament, these individuals were anointed to do the assignments that God had given them to build the temple. With the Holy Spirit being with us to influence, inspire, help, there are anointed individuals in our own lives that God has called to help us to accomplish the plan.

That's how serious God is about us perpetually succeeding. God is not setting us up for failure. I want that to sit with you for a minute, and let it resonate and get in your spirit. God does not set us up for failure. If God has given us a plan, He wants us to perpetually succeed.

He's given us that divine download because He desires that we succeed. God is not setting us up to fail, but we have to know when it's time to pass the plan along, just as David knew to do.

It's as if he knew the anointing had moved from him. God had given it to him, and he birthed the part of it that he was supposed to birth. Then he shared the plans with Solomon, who gave them to his son. Some things are for us to see through completion, and some things are just for us to break the ground.

Think about a point in your life when it was time to move on to something else, but you stayed too long and wore out your welcome. God doesn't want us to wear out our welcome. We've got to know when it's time to pass the plan along. That's how we perpetually succeed. Often, when it's time for us to pass something else along, it's because He wants to give us another assignment or project – another divine download.

Chapter 13

Realize Success

*N*ow we go onto the last step of how to B.S. your way to success. You're here! You have arrived! You did it! You are at the place where you are realizing success. You are making it happen. You did the hard work, you did the heavy lifting, and here it is.

Belief systems require a shift to serve your shine. A successful person made it to their destination, whether anybody else knows it or not. They had to move forward on their own and encourage themselves to do the necessary work, the same work that you're doing by participating reading this guide.

My daughter and I realized success for us. We finally made the trip to Dubai to celebrate a milestone year for my daughter and I. We both celebrated milestone birthdays. I will turn fifty this year, and I promised her that when she turned thirty, if she was still single, we would go to Dubai.

I was in Dubai twice in two years, once at the end of 2019 and again at the start of 2020. I wanted to enjoy all of the culture that they had to offer. So, when it was time to get on the camel, I was a little scared. I said: "Oh my gosh, am I going to fall off?" But I didn't. I made all the necessary adjustments because I knew I wanted to enjoy every morsel of Dubai. There I was on a camel by myself and had a blast. When it was time to get off, I was scared again, but I had the experience. I realized success because that's what success looked like for me at that particular moment.

What came up for you as your read about "realize success?" Make a list here of belief systems that manifest you realizing the success you desire. This is your safe space. I'm not even going to limit you with lines. Just let it flow and pour out onto the page.

Chapter 14

S.H.I.N.E.

At this point in the process we have dealt with our mind-set. We've taken a magnifying glass to our thinking. How we think about ourselves, our circumstances, our strengths, and our abilities has come full circle. We've got our coming-out wardrobe and mindset. Nothing and no one can stop us but ourselves. We are in agreement with where we are and where we want to be. No stopping us now.

We have found our zone and are realizing success in a beautiful and wholesome way.

That gets us in a position to S.H.I.N.E. our boss belief system. We now

Show-up, Honestly, Intentionally, No Excuses.

Put it all on display. Showcase the gift of the successful you to the world. The best version of Y-O-U!

S.H.I.N.E

| SHOW UP |
| HONESTLY |
| INTENTIONALLY |
| NO |
| EXCUSES |

5
REALIZE
SUCCESS

MANIFEST

Mind

Guidepost Four

Chapter 15

Journey Strengths

*I*n the overview, I promised that the chapters wouldn't be too long. This may be the shortest chapter in the book.

While I was getting my Women's Executive Leadership certificate from the Brookings Institution, I had to take the VIA Character Survey and the Gallup Strengthsfinder. For context, the Brookings Institution is a nonprofit public policy organization based in Washington, DC. Their mission is to conduct in-depth research that leads to new ideas for solving problems facing society at the local, national, and global level.

The benefit of taking these surveys was to inform us of the strengths that we bring to the table; professional and personal. Research has proven that when working to achieve life goals from a position of strength, the chances to be successful increases exponentially. Whereas it was found that trying to turn weaknesses into strengths is not only frustrating but significantly hinders ones' ability to reach desired goals and successes.

Success achievement is not for the weak. It takes strength, fortitude, sacrifice, and stick-to-itiveness. Knowing my strengths has served me so well both professionally and personally that I incorporate the VIA Character Survey in my coaching practice.

As I have mention often throughout the blueprint, I am here to help you. You may take the 100% free VIA Character Strength Survey at this link:

https://bsbreakthroughsession.pro.viasuvey.org

Although there are twenty-four strengths in total, you will receive your top five-character strengths. The first five are your default or go-to strengths.

If you would like to have a quick group B.S. Boss Breakthrough Session with me to go over your number one strength and how to use it with The B.S. Boss Blueprint you may sign up at this link:

https://bit.ly/EABRKTHRU

Chapter 16

Let Us Pray

*G*od, as we sigh a sigh of relief, as we exhale each breath, we breath out the old. We release what was, to embrace what is to come. We thank you for order and process. We are grateful for the examples of people that have come before us in this journey called life.

We stand in agreement with each guidepost that you have provided us to believe, create, and manifest the life that our heart desires. We activate the law of agreement with the steps to build a solid foundation and pillars to get us to the place of realizing success.

Hear our prayer, God, for each step of the way. We thank you now for helping us and allowing us to partner with you to make it happen.

Believe

Oh Lord God, we thank you. We give you glory and honor for what you declare and decree to us as an example in Jeremiah 29. Lord God, we thank you that you have a plan, that you, first and foremost, you are God and you know what you're doing. You are in control from beginning to the end. You don't start anything that you can't finish. God, because you are God and you know what you are doing, we thank you for the plan that you plotted from beginning to end. You are the Alpha and the Omega, the beginning and the end, and the God of the in-between too. Lord God, we thank you that also said that you would take care of us, that you will not abandon us, that you are there for us, and that you are looking out for us, and that is your plan. We glorify you for that.

Lord God, Father God, we thank you. We bless your name, that you will give us the desire and the thing that we hope for and fulfill that thing and see it come to pass. That is what you desire, to give us that thing that we hope for. We bless your name, oh God. We glorify you, Lord God. We thank you now and we decree it as so. Forgive us, God, for shorting you. Forgive us for not giving you all the proper honor and glory for knowing what you're doing. We thank you. We submit to your plan, your vision in gold, Lord God. We thank you, Father, for giving us the desire of our heart. We thank you for the plan for us to perpetually succeed. Oh, glory to God. Thank you, God. Thank you, God. Thank you, God.

Create

God, we thank you. I thank you for those who are reading *The Blueprint* today. I thank you that it is not by mistake, that you wanted them to know that you are there. You have a plan for them to perpetually succeed. You have a plan to turn everything around for them that has been done, to turn evil against them around for their good. That you have a desire to bless them so that they can bless others.

And that you have a desire to heal their heart, Lord God, so that they can be healing, hope and love in the earth, Lord God. So that they can demonstrate that to someone else.

I decree and declare perpetual success for them right now in the name of Jesus. I thank God for each and every one of them, Lord God. Let them know. Encourage their hearts, oh God. Let them know that I am here as your instrument, as your tool, as your oracle, Lord God, to share with them and pray on their behalf. In Jesus' name we pray. Amen.

Manifest

God, I thank You for the individual that is reading this book. I thank You for that man. I thank You for the woman. I thank You for that child.

I thank You for the millennial, Lord God. I thank You for the individual that wanted to throw in the towel for thinking that they are a failure, or thinking and trying to be deceived by the enemy that You somehow have left them and forgotten about them. God, I thank You, that You have a plan for us. You have a plan for us to perpetually succeed, oh God. I thank You, that You have encouraged our souls in part one, in part two, in part three, Lord God. I thank You, God, that we are taking these nuggets of truth, that we are taking the word, and we are holding You accountable to keep Your word.

You have declared in Your word that You watch over Your word to perform it. Lord God, we set this word at Your feet. We ask, God, that You make it come to pass. We know that You are the same yesterday, today, forever. We know that You don't lie, that You are a promise keeper, You are true to Your word, and You have given us three different examples, three illustrations of Your children that You have caused to succeed in spite of famines, in spite of loss, in spite of setbacks, Lord God. We've got an example that You are a God of repeat performances, oh God. Thank You for repeating the performance in our life, oh God.

Thank You for the plan for us to perpetually succeed. We give You glory, Lord God. We thank You, in Jesus' name. Amen, amen, and amen.

Thank you so much for joining me. I thank God for you, and I thank God, and now, you've got a three-part plan on how to perpetually succeed.

Chapter 17

Now W.I.N.!!!!

Whatever
Is
Necessary
W.I.N.
I love an acronynm!

*W*henever it's necessary, wash, rinse, and repeat the four steps to get to the success you desire.

It's important to always be reassessing, renovating, redefining, and reaffirming in order to get to the place of realizing success. What does success look like to you? What does it feel like? What does it smell like? What does it taste like? What do you need to change and how do you need to shift your belief system? Go through those four steps again, because I promise that when you do that, you will get to the place where you realize success.

You have no choice. It's just like ABC – realizing success is to grasp or understand clearly; to make real or give reality to; to bring vividly to mind. It is real to you. When I say you have no choice, I mean that once you follow all those steps, you will realize success is just like getting promoted to the next grade.

You do the work at those various levels, and there's no choice but for you to be promoted. And you're able to do all of that, and then some!

About the Author

Dr. Lisa Lewis Ellis is The Belief System (B.S.) Boss because belief systems require a S.H.I.F.T. to S.E.R.V.E. your unique S.H.I.N.E.! Dr. Lisa teaches how to achieve success by releasing the mental restraints of self-limiting belief systems. She is a certified John Maxwell Team coach, international speaker, teacher, trainer, best-selling author, and the founder of Kick Boxing Believers, L.L.C. With thirty-one years and counting of leadership and management experience, Dr. Lisa is well equipped to serve you and your organization.

She has been seen in *Kivo Daily, MSN, Praise 107.9, Spirit 1340, Black Enterprise, The New York Times, Sheen Magazine, Chicago Tribune, Huffpost, Fox News, ABC, CEO Blog Nation, Fupping, Lifeology,* and many more!

30 Years of Leadership & Management in the Public Sector (Budget and Finance)

MizCEO Society for Coaches Executive Coaching Certification
Certificate in Public Leadership (The Brookings Institute)
Certificate in Personal Development & Executive Coaching (The CaPP Institute)
Ordained Elder/Clergy (Christian)
The President's Lifetime Achievement Award 2018

Humanitarian Award 2018 (Trinity International University of Ambassadors, Atlanta, GA)
Honorary Doctor of Divinity (Trinity International University of Ambassdors, Atlanta, GA)
High Definition Woman Magazine Inaugural Issue Honoree 2018

Phone: (833) 542-2697
Email: lisa@lisalewisellis.com
Website: www.LisaLewisEllis.com
Facebook: www.facebook.com/LisaLewisEllis
Twitter: www.twitter.com/LisaLewisEllis
Instagram: www.instagram.com/LisaLewiEllis
YouTube: www.bit.ly/YouTubeLisaLewisEllis
LinkedIn: www.linkedin.com/in/LisaLewisEllis
Periscope: http://www.periscope.tv/LisaLewisEllis

www.ingramcontent.com/pod-product-compliance
Lightning Source LLC
Chambersburg PA
CBHW060533030426
42337CB00021B/4246